DISCLAMOR

DISCLAMOR

Poems by
G.C. Waldrep

AMERICAN POETS CONTINUUM SERIES, NO. 106

BOA Editions, Ltd. ❧ Rochester, NY ❧ 2007

First Edition
07 08 09 10 7 6 5 4 3 2 1

Publications and programs by BOA Editions, Ltd.—a not-for-profit corporation under section 501 (c) (3) of the United States Internal Revenue Code—are made possible with the assistance of grants from the Literature Program of the New York State Council on the Arts; the Literature Program of the National Endowment for the Arts; the County of Monroe, NY; the Lannan Foundation for support of the Lannan Translations Selection Series; the Sonia Raiziss Giop Charitable Foundation; the Mary S. Mulligan Charitable Trust; the Rochester Area Community Foundation; the Arts & Cultural Council for Greater Rochester; the Steeple-Jack Fund; the Elizabeth F. Cheney Foundation; Eastman Kodak Company; the Chesonis Family Foundation; the Ames-Amzalak Memorial Trust in memory of Henry Ames, Semon Amzalak and Dan Amzalak; and contributions from many individuals nationwide. See Colophon on page 104 for special individual acknowledgments.

Cover Design: Prime8Media
Cover Art: "Infantry (for Leon Golub)" by Irving Petlin
Interior Design and Composition: Richard Foerster
BOA Logo: Mirko

Library of Congress Cataloging-in-Publication Data

Waldrep, George Calvin, 1968–
    Disclamor : poems / by G.C. Waldrep. — 1st ed.
        p. cm. — (American poets continuum series ; no. 106)
    ISBN 978–1–929918–97–3 (pbk.)
    I. Title.

PS3623.A358D57 2007
811'.6—dc22
                                    2007008021

BOA Editions, Ltd.
Nora A. Jones, Executive Director/Publisher
Thom Ward, Editor/Production
Peter Conners, Editor/Marketing
Glenn William, BOA Board Chair
A. Poulin, Jr., President & Founder (1938–1996)
250 North Goodman Street, Suite 360
Rochester, NY 14607
www.boaeditions.org

NATIONAL
ENDOWMENT
FOR THE ARTS

State of the Arts
NYSCA

Contents

But what can I say about the swamp I came to? About the laughter?
The animals I brushed against and the murmur of invisible things?

—Max Jacob

Cloud of Witnesses

Day's cage again and this time I try for a breeze,
I open a window to the east and a window to the west and I think
that this is something like the holly that lifts its blood-
fruit bright to the morning sun, to the afternoon sun,
to the evening breeze though with less fervor,
and I think the phone will ring. It always has. It is not ashamed of this,
its function, like the hollyberries in their naked plenty
which bob and weave, the bees which,
seeking their gilded herm, their bone-skep pene-
trate and stop at one single point, as light in certain media.
I crave the aftersilence. Angry buzz as night falls:
that artificial sun, a carnegie of lovers. I had rather been weeping.
It is beautiful. It is almost fearfully beautiful.
It is most fearsomely beautiful. I am still thinking, I am still waiting
for the phone to ring. The holly plays host to its spare nation.
If I believed you what would change. Tell me.

Battery Rathbone-McIndoe

—So many ways I could begin.

There is history: built 1905, decommissioned 1948,
    guns (four, each 6" in diameter)
        sold for scrap.
There is nomenclature:
    2nd Lt. Samuel B. Rathbone,
        killed War of 1812,
    Maj. Gen. James McIndoe,
                slain in France, 1918.

To the east, Upper Fisherman's Beach,
    pale bodies against black sand.
To the west, Point Bonita's vigil.
And the south tower of the bridge, its harp, its
    iron mandolin curding the city
        into strips, grey, vertical,
            gleaming—

Can you believe I once stood for war?
    (Can you believe I once stood against it?)

In the narrows, a lone sailboat.
    Late rain for the season.
        Uncommon to see a sailboat out this far.

It moves slowly, from left to right,
   as if trying to say something
     very precise,
  and then again, from right to left,
     as if erasing.

East pillbox: APATHETIC YOUTH,
    roots of words
      ancient in two cultures.
But there is also OKSANA, 9/23/00.
   CITY OF INGLEWOOD, CA!
    DON L/S MELISSA,
     JESSICA & JOE,
       SAUL + YOLANDA.

   MY GIRLFRIEND BLED HERE.

In smaller letters,
    NO WAR ON ANYBODY.
  Smaller yet:
    I AM GOD.

    West pillbox, unmistakable
      smell of urine.

Black spray paint:
  IVONNE JOSÉ KARLA DANIEL
  4/22/99.

ED + SONIA,
NANCY ♥ JESÚS.
In chalk, baby blue
   with yellow highlights:
      "Love Your Family & Nature."
  (Underneath, neatly printed
     in what looks like Wite-Out:
           WHY?)

One by one the barges, like small planets,
   socket past, below the bridge and into the harbor.
     They take their time.

Steel rivet of sky,
     horizon's bulkhead.

           Some say
   trade is like war, only slower.

Natural history; or,
   the more successful invasions:
     miner's lettuce, coreopsis,
         Hottentot fig.

I walked here, there were
    no guns, no gates, now
      everything is permitted.
No one had sold the sand in my shoes.
No one has yet tasted his death

on my tongue,

this is *before*

as there must always be *before*

(just as what comes next

is *after*—)

Bloom of the blue-eyed grass.
Soak of an April squall.

West pillbox
((further yet, as if in answer))—

THE BLACK DOG RUNS BY NIGHT.

Evensong:
All Eyes Sharper

Not easily:
the field or the forcep.

The saint in his pine box says nothing.

Not the light tracing
the curve of a doe's neck
at evening.
Not the evening.

O eros.

Not the delicate filigree
rather the bucket
up from its well of deep feeling.
Not the feeling, but
the bucket.
The moss of it, a growing
thing but slowly.

Not the friction, not the hand.

To be led

eros, arras, errare .

O let me not be a worker.
O
the vegetable sun,

a nickel for the sun's child
in the marketplace! O the wine,
ringing its carafe.

The saint in his pine box says nothing.

O I am first
by the look of you.

Every Apple, Every
Dreamer, Every Prime

At the top of the stairs: a horse. No,
the shadow of a horse. No: a shadow

as if cast by stair: if cast: (that is,
thrown): as if recollection. Mete answer,

virginal smutch. Dependent on skill:
mine. Or another's. And like a bronze

monument. No need to defend; as if
we were going: somewhere, same place

electricity goes at night. The sound
it makes: I am always confusing

with blood: (the sound): that purling
hum. A plaque to mark where the village

stood. Obscured by snow. As if a
form had lingered: hesitant, or drawn:

no matter. With my nickeled key
I'm unlocking the door. With my good

eye I am scanning: the landing: no
horses here. I'm promised. *Cast*

your thread upon the waters. In terms
of the scaffold, in terms of the lave.

The spit or the serry. Add vellum, brush
away the old equations: Archimedes

displaced. Were it so easy to remember.
The sire and the dam, the field

laced with honey. A scarab of bees.
Where I bought him. Without impediment

this pine threshold. No: chipped from
residence. As preference: sweet acre.

There is always a spy wanting to see
                              what you see.
There is always one spy, wanting.

City in Search of a Death

At first there was no evident logic. You garlanded the hills—hibiscus & rosemary—while I scrubbed down the flagstones with vinegar.

Now, a destroyer cruises offshore in the middle distance.

My job is to make a circuit of smoky bars and video arcades, reprogramming the dialogue. Instead of blows each pixel will trade Dickinson for Nietzsche, Whitman for Weil.

There's a caffeine smog this morning so thick traffic deadlocks, each driver imbibing through the skin. This is how the city stays awake.

By the harbor Koreans & Japanese are arguing the appearance of 19th-century schooners. They have been at this a long time. We stop for a bit, empty our pockets of loose change to watch the deliberations.

When the spaces between us get too wide we pretend it is our own ghosts we are hunting.

Remember our arrival: the breechcloth, the calfskin binding. You did not walk away from the signature my body opened. Peering into our suite—the Crazy Horse Special, so sparsely furnished—you said you were glad the gods had long ago taken sides.

I have been issued two keys, one ivory, one gold. Be patient. I have not yet renounced what I shall renounce.

The branches burn bright because I've set the tree on fire.

Battery Wallace

A turn—to the left—
    it is day again, the habitations of men
        spill from cliff to beach,
    from partridge to kestrel
            across the narrows:

Possession. And rife
    with report of our frailties,
                myriad.

AND THE GOD OF USA DECLARED
        I SHALL INCORPORATE WEAPONS
                OF MASS DESTRUCTION
        INTO MY NATIONAL PARKS.

—This is not quite right. The weapons came first,
        mass, the destruction; then
            picnic tables.

Built in 1919 as an open firing platform.
        Rebuilt 1942, casemated
                with reinforced concrete ceilings
                    covered by earth
        and camouflaging vegetation.

Abandoned, 1948.

The 12" coastal rifles
> were intended to duel with battleships
>> seventeen miles at sea.

In the round of the south casemate:
> E.T. IS HERE.
> NORM LOVES DREW BARRYMORE
>> AND JULIA SCHULTZ.
> WAR ROOM.
> ETERNAL LOVE!
> ART = FAITH = PROMOTION.
> D-DAY 9/12/02

>> —a woman's candystriped panties;
>>> a sketch of Point Bonita

and its lighthouse
> rendered passably   in charcoal
>> on the plastered wall.

>> *Night. I dream*
> *there exists a maturity apart from place,*
>> *like picking berries*

from these sharp canes.
God doesn't mind.
> *The juice stains my palms.*

I want to be humane, but in my heart
> *nineteenth-century Californians*
keep telling yellow peril jokes.

Why?

—to keep Him enthralled?
　　　—within the drama of representations?
　　　　　—or for some other purpose?

What I meant:
　　　　that there is volition
　　as there must also be consequence.

We make an industry of beauty.
　　See, here, the crank, the dripping
　　　　flange. The lupine,
　　　　　　the paintbrush, the harlequin:

　　incorporated:

And wanting, at last, to know

　　　　　　　　that other, that
　　underneath—

　　　　　　I drop a coin.
　　　It echoes in the shaft.
　My refusal.

The Little Man in the Fire Hates Me

There is not so much water here as pollen.

A lesson in obedience, in Victorian industry:
I am busy, busy   therefore the child will live.
Sheets blossoming like crucified roses.
I beg the silk of a single petal. Am denied.
You will not need this currency for your particular journey.

I return to the stove.
The boiling pot is neither abstract nor demure.
It is hissing its elementary decalogue.

True: I am embarrassed by the fact of the book.
False: I regret it.

Sometimes I linger, sometimes not.
No cries come from the next room.
But I am still trying to believe. The incarnation, the thrust.
And what becomes of that other.
Exhausted. Viviparous.
Salt rising like a buzz from the invection.
A lowering.

Everyone wants to fuse a tragic story to his own, after the fact.

bergamot, turk's cap, spiderwort, yarrow, foamflower
(fire-pink dying—
(pink orchids, where you waited—

There is a third cell in the eye that witnesses to the light.
When voice fails, the body substitutes.

Candlemas, Vermont

As in the interval between speech we labored.
Some insecurity about the text, about the tumescence
of old maps, their garish color schemes, their X's
ocellate, marking spots. And so to the mouse-riddled tenement
with its poked screens and sagging gambrels.
And finding a path we said adieu
to the mice, who watched us from the hollows of their hollow
teeth. Behind and away from the habitation
our feet sank into something like pine.
It was strange, walking on that which had been part
of something so vertical, so extraneous
to our own notions of reproduction, of sex.
But soft like that, and pointed where the water had not
yet done its work. And we saw them from a distance, at first
a patch here, a patch there, a milkiness
on the surface of the needles. And sight should have
interfered with speech but did not. Should have
consecrated narrative but did not. So much buying & selling,
so many doves in the cages of the marketplace, so
many top-40 hits. And we were coming
up on the whiteness of their white the way a ship moves
out from dry dock into the small patch of water
that is masquerading as ocean. "Ocean"
unlike "water" being a fiction, a figment, a figure
to believe in. We collude
in these, our bodies, and what we
think of as the sea calls to them, what we think of
as the moon calls to what we think of as the sea
in the short circuit of the flesh.

And then we were on top of them, by which I
mean among them, we could see the lithe
and horny stalks, the delicate belling,
Indian pipe, corpse plant.
And there were thousands of them, tens of
thousands, as there should not have been, among the needles.
And there was no narrative in this so that eventually
even the interval between speech fell silent
before the prospect of finding that for which one had not known
one was searching. As if the tenement behind us
had become a villa for silence, larger silences and smaller,
procreative and adolescent silences all dwelling
beneath the same eaves and growing more
silent together. And the mice would be servants to that
greater silence, wouldn't they, you said.
Wouldn't they, you said. *To which court resort for succor*
is what I thought. And so speech is a homeless thing
like a map drained of its pigments.
I had not believed. As if
my unbelief could save me, or anything, as if
by lying down beneath the pines I could have had a part
in that deafchant. And the path kept going,
deeper into the wood, though we went no further that day.
And the mice slept in the tenement of their own small silences,
and the berry canes withheld their counsel. Lear said
nothing comes of nothing. *Speak again.*

Circle Park

At the place in the trail where one is supposed
to leave a stone, I take one. Selfish, I know, but I reckon
it confers another *nostos*, more or less.
And what a view! Charred hemlocks at horizon's lip,
gurgle of snowmelt two seasons up.
I'm told that soon my breath will start to come short
on account of the altitude. I've read about this, been waiting
for it all my life. Breathing is the one thing I do well,
except when it interferes with sleeping.

I remember the way the children filed in
clutching their pillows, shyly, a nervous giggle
somewhere in the vicinity of the old RCA television's
dark paneling. My idea was
anyone who fell asleep in the next hour
probably needed the rest. I turned down the lights,
let the vanguard get comfortable. In the story I told,
every part of the body was on speaking
terms with every other part, a perfect conversation
that preceded an elevator's assured rise to surface.
One by one the children stepped away

just in time to see a stag leaping a bank of horsetail ferns.
Breathe deeply, I told them, and they did.
They had given up the idea of their own bodies
or rather their bodies had given up the idea
of being *them*, for the moment. Maybe for the last time.
I spoke softly about the ubiquity
of granite schist, about the importance of understanding Mozart

as both a found object and a syntax. Soon they were still;
I was alone. My last lung had already sailed.

Bergson's Arrow

Rain in the holly, rain on the
                              shelf of self.
Many things may be blamed on the fall line:
        the mechanization of flour
        and weapons production, the rise
                        and ultimate wreckage
of Richmond's Jackson Ward.
        A surgical procedure was pending:
        I had developed
striations in the passageways of my
        incli-

                nations,
        stress fractures
along the waterfront vistas
                              of semblance,
        those pleasing prospects, those
                        gay promenades.
No further tickets would be issued,
        no more booths at the Tri-County Fair
                nor natives on the far shore
waiting to express
        their complete confidence
                        in what could only
        be degrading.
        A clearer praxis
                        would *involve,*
        e.g., turn in on itself
& then away. There should, perhaps,
be a museum of numbers

here, at the liminal juncture,
             in place of this museum
of trains & palaces. We have not received
             any coded messages.
             The possibility of love remains
    real
             though relegated to foot-
                            notes, first
    physician of race & gender:
Heal thyself. Some implement
                     drawn from the suture
                            (again).
    To stay on the subject. To be
             thrown under, and yet remain.

Battery Mendell

This is become a place of children.

I squat, and with the muscles of my calves
      suspend my rhythm
                —the dirge, the waltz—
      over these sea-cliffs.

Inheritance, then:
        that which cannot be refused;
        that which is beyond purchase;
        that which is a given,

                  given.

The mustard, the tansy, the sea-fig,
      the tolling of the buoys—

Let us agree, for the moment, that this
      is a religion. Let us imagine
        these shrines
    in the guise they now assume:
           superaltar, amphitheater,
      ERIC + STACY,

          GINA L/S WADE.

(And what they assume
        we shall assume: these are the rules
              of this game.)

In one story,
        it is a child that calls to each of us
          in his time,

from a low stone wall.
        A cut-up. A mimic.
                His salt is our salt.
        His hair is the wheat

        we grind for bread.
           —Have you not heard this story?
Could it be possible
        you have never heard it?

                —In one version,
      this child had a brother.

I rise as the children run
        up and down the catwalks,
      along the concrete galleries.

They are delighted, they ask
      "Can we *really* go in here?"
             They wait

for condemnation
    as we wait for mercy.

How they blaze with their small fires!
    They are the warnings we ignore,
        the beacons.
They are so hot now we cannot touch them.
    They will not be held.
    They turn as this world turns,

      as the cormorant, as the gull,
      all life
dives within hunger—

That window.

        I hear

the rushing of the wave.

Blood Ruminant

When one is a child one cannot tell
Calvary from cavalry, the hill
for the horsemen. Each means your death.
Letters are trees.
Behind them something
walks, or struggles. You strain to see
just what sort of beast this is.
Not a nice one, perhaps. Not like
the sleeping kitten,
or the Sunday school lambs.
There may be an army in the forest
and not kind at all.
A nick in the lead-based paint.
Or the soldiers themselves, soft & heavy.
Something walks behind them
and it might be language.
Language, the adults hiss, at the older boys
and girls with their musky scents, some-
times at each other.
As if what is hidden
comes to light, in this forest.
And if the figures be melted down, cast
& sharpened—   *Here*
is the church, and here
is the steeple.
The fingers inside blind.
Like the alphabet.
You add eyes—twin pricks—to the
O, to the e. And stand

corrected. Smooth, yes, as a trunk, yes.
As the seam of a soldier.
Will I make a good one, you wonder. Just then,
beyond your range of vision, something
moves. Careful
aim. In the distance a bald hill.
Bare. Someone or something has left it.
A loamy odor, as of shirts
worn by men.
And you hear the baying, no
the neighing of the horses.
The one with the black mane is the one
you like best.
It is a blind horse, but powerful.
It has thrown its rider.
Wounded, he has hidden himself. In the forest.
From which you cannot tear your
error. Or the barrel of your toy musket.
Your own lips moving. By way of
invitation. Or reply.

The Resurrection: Sweden

The idea that there is such a thing as the elemental
is an old one. Why resist?
There's fire, and then there's water. Earth and sky,
Simon says. At the center of the park a scale model of a ceremonial
    kiva, sealed
except for one secret entrance the carnies use for smokes.
They've been taking my money all day
and I'm tired of it.
Every seduction duplicates a gesture
the real world vends for free:
vertigo, weightlessness, the texture of corduroy
on an autumn night somewhere downstate, in the sticks,
with the lights coming on
the same way they are right now.
I can hear them laughing.
I'm tired of it. Bursting through the sod & stucco won't help.
Remembering that Marsden Hartley sketched the two crucified
    thieves
as a bodybuilder & a clown comes closer,
only his Christ had no face.
Hartley was, essentially, a landscape painter
who remembered, periodically, how much water there was in the
    human body.
He was ugly. He liked garish colors.
All summer he cruised the county fairs of Maine.
His brutalized Christ had no face.

Hotel d'Avignon

The religious cry in their patois of sand and dusk.
If I could find the portico I would repaint the columns.
No one has left the key with me
so I sketch one on scratch paper.
I am a handy artist, so this is easy:
the notches are precise, there is a sense
of perspective in the hatching of the brass,
as from a light source.
Through the corridors I walk
with my paper key held before me.
Night is always the same here. Outside
the religious fragment slowly into the tall grasses:
my paper key is a fine instrument
and yet they are afraid of it.
All night, from their crusts of earth,
the religious mutter curses: They hope I will lose the key,
that I will crumple or erase it, at least
that I will never use it.
Listen, I call to them through the grille,
Everything in the world is a knife,
everything in the world cuts a little from you.
But they do not listen. I do not speak their language.
Through the night as through the day
I walk, perform small tasks.
Some days I think about drawing a new key.
Some days I do.
Light is untidy, my mother used to say, clucking gently.
You must collect the rays scattered about you.

Titus at Lystra

To bring the curious to heal.
A conic section: parabola? Ellipse?
A vesicle conscripted from the oriflamme,
rejecting, rejected,
a butchered
iridescence on the Schuylerville pike.
There was no time to form
a judgment, no instinct for order, to reflect
that rage was an option: that,
independent of the banefire, absolution
might lie further
than mercy was prepared
to go. And so off the pommel at moonset.
And so slope working
its way into the land like flour
into oil: more like oil, the slick of it:
hands fastened
in a chain that resembled
nothing so much as singing, angle
of a mouth
wide open, corners
where lip-flesh never quite reached—
where the tongue seeks,
as if conveying balm, and the chap cankers
in the incarcerate light, body
homing into body,
the nape of that moment
set like a sapphire into the scepter
of incident, smooth and cool.

A vestment of measure.
To dowse for that secret spring:
the geese,
the temblor, what
livid farrowing. And turned again
into the preparation, its vast appointments.
A crossing made once. In
strength. In summer.

Battery O'Rorke

What is written here fades quickly.
    Faces drawn in chalk,
        names,
                    the idea
    of defense, of a beach
            ripe for landing.

West, east, the longitudes of war.
    This is no place for monuments.

If I had ever doubted
    then *hid* for *cry*, *gill* for *gull*
        and the incision
    a careless thing,
           stain of interval.

I walked to the sea as I walk to the sea,
    I am a creature of the sea
        as I am also its fastness,
           its sharp holt.

The sea is a conspirator of great forgiveness,
    it is the cardamom of waters.

It is a mistake to suppose one's self lonely.
I carry the bones of the pedagogue
                    in ivory brackets,
        my hand is steady,
                I mix consecration
                            with consecration.

                Still I want:

the body of that other,
            the magnitude, the chalice.

The beach is the ocean's daughter,
            she dances on her diagonal
                            in the moonlight.

There will always be some
                who take pleasure
        in what the body can be made to do:

The playing of the lute.
                The marathon, the obeisance,
        the pestle, fitted to its mortar.
                        The Catherine wheel.
                        The bascule.

(I want as I have always wanted.
        I think I must be a very minor poet,
            to want so—)

The beach ignores the power of words
as words ignore the power of things.

O stranger.

Transubstantiation Rag

I wanted to hide the fear that governs a single man,
that results in an economy of immense reparation, that is,
loneliness, let us allow that such existed,
that it weighed only a few ounces,
that it occupied a varying volume
(as ostrich feathers or greed) expanding or contracting
according to pressure, that it required no external power source,
that it was not seething, that it could be worn
as a garment—or as jewelry—let us assume I wore it
so that what it covered was easily deduced by the observer
but known with certainty only to myself,
or not even me, let us assume
that the very idea gave me pleasure, and gives,
the way the hand of a paraclete dares—
probes—extends—let us suspect
that I am prone to fits of retributive thinking, that I have walked
out into the night on occasion and shaken my fist
at the moon, let us presume that on such occasions
I was dressed appropriately, or not,
let us concede the possibility of cold fusion
(though likewise a fifth and perfect chamber for the heart),
I am not accustomed to interruption
so let me finish this particular geometry
the way a constellation would but with less
mythic clutter and a more practical rate of exchange,
let us cast aside all reasonable doubt,
pierce hot metal with holes for nails
and plunge into cold water,
let us inhale the steam as it binds flesh to bone,

let us embrace the wilderness of one metaphysical conceit
though every copse hides
its adder, its Indian, its free-trade zone,
let us suspect that this is inevitable (and for good reason),
let us appreciate the elegance of the *ecorché*
but mark the smile, lips parted slightly,
eyes mischievous, let us believe that without the tongue
the retinas would pace indefinitely, no
morbid corrective—and motives in the balance—
let us posit an exchange of rings
though by faith this heirloom has served well,
let us consider the prosperity of the Cultivator of Vistas,
the utility of the snath,
let us introduce a ceremony of twigs and latchets,
let us admit that everyone stumbles, now and again, and some
fall, though we are fixed to this earth,
let us count the cost, *if you leave this place in freedom*
are you not the richer master—

Hall of Ancestors

There's a father and the father is dying. Or, there's a father and the father is dead. Or, there's a father in the poem who is either dying or is already dead, or there is a father who objects to the fact of the poem, would object to the facts of the poem, has objected, will object.

Outside the hall of smoked mirrors a whistle blows, the same sort of steam whistle that used to mark shift changes at factories. No one pays it any attention. Everyone inside the hall reads the smoked mirrors the way you might read a book. Instead of turning pages they change mirrors. In this way they move through the maze at a more or less orderly pace.

There exists a precise dramatic interval during which all the possible yous resolve into a single you, frequently a you, a particular you, that had not ranked, not visibly, among the acknowledged possibilities. Begging questions of which god, which machine. Also of vantage.

At the point where the heroine runs from the palisade of thatched huts, tears screaming down her face, sandals lost in the tropical mud, we think, *You should have known this was coming.* We did. We knew it was coming, and yet we kept watching/reading. The palm wine, the bits of seared flesh that might have been chimpanzee, the woman who might or might not have been the sub-minister's village wife. . . .

We keep reading. Consequently the water for tea boils over, into the hissing dahlia of the gas flame. Accusations follow, a row threatens. *You should have known this was coming.*

The ashes of the father may be entered into any available vessel, then placed appropriately among the effects of the living. Bookshelf as columbarium. Dovecote, garden plot, astrolabe.

The more outlandish the vessel the better, especially if the end result is scripted as comedy or farce.

Late into the night translators work over the texts left by the French poets. The translators, like the poets and their texts, are haunted. From their long desks they look to each other fearfully; they rub their aching limbs. The house is dark and getting darker. It wasn't supposed to be like this. It wasn't supposed to be like this at all.

Romeward

Or, failing that, a bathetic intervention
at Melita. Those primitive tribes! The hurly-
burly, beating of skin-tight drums
around the bonfire—

I would have followed you
there, would have stolen passage
on that same ship, weathered that same storm.
And cast out upon that same sea

the fourteenth night—I would have counted—
suspicion of anchorage, fear of rending
in night's shive, I too would have
"wished for the day";

from the hull of that galley
with rock for hair and sand for skin
(like wheat cast into current)   I too
would have taken counsel

with the others, to spare your life,
knowing that on the island the serpent waited.
Such kindness, pyreside. Man's
thirst for first-blush—

Who would not have taken your rough hand?
Who would not have poisoned you?

What Lived in Our Mouths

At first there were small bats, dropping
like teeth at the onset of evening, warm and furry.
But their leathery wings tickled
our palates. Next
a clutch of scarab beetles,
which climbed down our flannel shirts
one by one in their stately and elegant way
in the mornings, and back
when the dew fell. After they left
a family of severed fingers took up residence
behind our tongues. We tasted
the salt of them, ghost-rime of their daily
occupations, their steep longing for the integral.
Whether they were all in exile
from the same body
or a collection of disparate, refugee digits
we never found out. After them
our mouths were vacant for a long season,
or so it seemed: we who had been used to such
company, so many kingdoms.

Battery Smith-Guthrie

Miwok in Miwok means "the people"
just as *the people* in the language of our people
    means "the people."

            This is convenient.

The purpose of images
        is to attract other images,
                one beside another,
                        above, beneath,
            eventually superseding.

Like attracts like.
        "One" is never large enough, nor "two."
        This is the story of life
                    as it is the story of death.

        This is also the story of naming.

        TIM + KHRISTINE
I LOVE IRISH.
        VIVA LA RAZA!
                    ERACISM.
        NAZIS SUCK
'69 MUSTANG CHARGER,

'72 TOYOTA.
ILLEGALLY SANE (AND LOVING IT).
I AM THE BONEMAN.
ANGELA LOVES ERNESTO.
NOT US!
YOU BE THE DEER.

Let us consider, then,
    the office of the guard,
        the treasurer, the hierophant,
      the lone policeman on his city beat.

Are they not like sunlight on this empty beach?
    Are they not bound, as we are?

In Miwok legend,
    there was a mysterious land
        far to the north:
    "wali-kapa was a sort of cliff or mountain.
      Beyond it the young ducks lived.
They said that on the other side
        the sky came way down.
   This land cannot be reached.
     Its passage is closed."

"Coyote tried to regulate the tides,
    but he had them so low
       most of the fish died.   Later,
          he corrected the error."

"The dead go toward Point Reyes.
  They say there is a little chunk of wood there
      which they use to make a fire.
    A piece of rock two feet long is at the spot
      where they jump into the ocean
            and then follow a road
                back of the breakers."

So the cup reclines

      from one hand to another.
So residence, so title.

     I mount no reasonable excuse.
This room was large enough already:
    through a clever acoustical trick
    I find that if I speak

        I can hear myself.

"In the early days, people didn't die.
   But Coyote wanted to hear people crying.
     He liked to listen to the noise. . . ."

Here there are no prizes, no awards,
      no dietary supplements.
Here there is only the ocean
   in flames.

Electuary

This is the easiest death I ever tried, shapeless
and comforting, something to strip from the body like a warm smell.
Sartre on Calder, 1946: *A mobile, we might say,*
is a little private celebration, an object defined by its movement
and having no other existence. Death is a story that only gets stranger:
the airwaves are in love with the soft down of our bodies
and tangle there, twining sweetly. Blocking traffic
would be one way to solve the problem
I've devised, a knee play in which light enters a room
at speed *x* and departs at speed *y*, in which a variant protein
ascends the ziggurat as a sort of stoop-shouldered suitor,
dimwitted but hopeful. At the top he shifts uneasily
from foot to foot. He knows if he looks down the world will end,
that his beloved in her dress of eyes will embrace
the inscrutability of a progressive enclosure. Jung aside
this could be the action I'm looking for,
the diffidence and the altitude. Far below
the river divorces yet again, leaving ox-bows on the plain.
At the Odeon everyone's watching the Jitterbug scene
from *The Wizard of Oz*, the giant spiders from *King Kong*,
an endless loop. These are the sorts of things we misplace
when we think everything's under control—father knows best—
nothin' says lovin' like something from the oven.
In the next world feminine mystique
will be a trademarked brand of writing paper. Meanwhile in this one
I'm beginning to feel a little worried, I want to step outside
into the topiaries and raise a placard to heaven that reads
WE'RE MAKING BABY FORMULA HERE,
just baby formula, each and every one of us are members

of an ancient and honorable guild, we are sorry,
we present the evidence of our contrition in a range of sober polymers.
A plastic bag catches and waves from a chain-link fence,
its gills pulsing weakly, out of their element.
I had not thought to feel weightless at this juncture,
so untethered. I'm putting on and taking off my clothes as fast as I can.
Last night at dinner someone asked me if I felt *relevant*.
What I want to know is, if I bend all my attention
to a single flaw, can I crack this crazy glass?

Appanage

For failure to trust
substitute a black house by steel tracks.
Inside a number of unrelated people,
men and women, are drowning.

The windows are high and grime-smeared.
I cannot see in.

Outside, on a heath
mottled by the shadows of passing clouds,
I attend to my assigned task.
I am, or was, the inventor of birds:

the kestrel and the cormorant,
the kea, the auk, and the sparrow.
To this day I believe I was very good at it.

At present I am only allowed
to use my hands. They make the heather
rustle with their umbras.

No one goes into the black house.
No one comes out.
Once in a while a long train
pulls through the cut, up the grade.

I flex my palms. Thumb to forefinger:
cockatoo. Three together: starling.

No one sees. I wonder if there were ever
any children in that house.

Bishopville

At the time I wanted nothing more
than to shrive what was left of that ghost town,
to beatify the tipples of those old mines.
I didn't mean that anyone needed to pray for them,
or to them: only that they were agents
of miracles. *You & the horse*
you strode in on. Might's chief avulsion
evoked the wingèd tribes—
birds avoided, bats dwelt there
rising at night in a way that suggested
yet another folktale about the origins of darkness.
I was living under a bridge
where the presence of a body—any body—
seemed to augur well. To drill into the procession
required a greater sense of social purpose
than I'd yet discovered.
Though I was invited to every vesper
I did not have the presence of mind to record
any of the major chants. The one about the bridge
was my favorite. Did it exist?
I wanted to interrupt: *Of course it does,*
I live beneath it. But did I really?
What was certain was that
the costermonger's habiliments were entirely
beyond my slender means. I tried speaking loudly
in the hope that this would suggest
my next rursus: primitive
echolocation. At this point Nietzsche's ghost
appeared to me in a dream.

We were waltzing, & discussing
how it was that a ghost could waltz,
but I couldn't make out Nietzsche's replies
because the orchestra was too loud.
Back under the bridge the bats were almost
certainly beginning their evening patrols.
I carried the plastic siphons with my bare hands.
Some felt there was still a chance
that marketable ore might be discovered
beneath the place where the angels
were said to have ascended, but I wasn't sure.
For one thing, they had been pretty tatty for angels.
I was all for arranging stones in circles
on Sky Butte, for letting *be* be.

Wunderkammern

I have lived in several worlds, all of them fine.
There was never any question of punishment, rather
representation of a like crystalline faith,
that the blower holds within herself
the unriddling ligature,
that the winter, pierce of ice, the snow
in its intricate fingering can be arrested, and hailed as beauty.
In this fashion the world remains with us.
I buy and I buy; with each receipt
something shredding and translucent breaks upward
from darkness. This is unavoidable.
With a light step and minimal violence I make
myself a tintype. As if invisible.
And thus escape that union.
I would rather, as some do, have left the road for the forest.
I would rather, as some do, bind the alternatives
and set them ablaze on a low hill.
Instead I raise a stone and leave my own
token in that cold place.
Each weight bears the memory of its slow burn,
its origin. What I am describing is what comes after.
I wanted to prolong the wishes, the wishing.
My patron turns in his slow flame.

Battery Alexander

But we are far from a capital city
    just as the Monterey cypress
        is far from its Monterey home.
            The capital lives in us,

    extinguished

   but sanguinary, sanguinary.
      This is the concealment, the deception:

As we live within the bounds of the capital
    the capital lives in us.

Down a flight of stairs.
    A cellar, a catacomb,
           a landing.
    A door. A grille
      and beyond that grille
        a perfumed garden.
   A maze of pipes. Or,
      nothing at all.

Question:
What is defense without a pretty view?

Answer: Geometry.

Eight mortars with snub barrels, 12" in diameter.

"These were designed specifically

to catapult shells in a high arc

onto the wooden decks of steel warships."

A meaning of intelligence:

in descent

the blind save their eyes

for the approaching flame.

Above, a hawk, harried

by a red-winged blackbird.

(Theirs is a private argument.)

Below, the hawk's prey,

everywhere.

During the tenure of my occupation

the only legible graffiti at Battery Alexander

read

PRO-DEATH NOW.

Down, then—

also

to be the object of desire.

Night.
In this dream I am a tour guide
      but I speak in some other language—
         I am the only one
   who does not understand
      the words I am saying.

At a long oak table I lift the lid
   of a tool box,
        remove each implement,
     explain its purpose.
Lay it aside.
   Move on to the next.

   With each
the crowd around me grows larger,
     more silent, more attentive.

      One after another
     I remove the tools from their box:
   the coulter, the adze,
     the iron hasp, fine gold strung
      like a pocket lyre.

We stand in a room with no windows.
   We stand this way for a long time.

     —Day again.
"Not that which goeth into the mouth
   defileth a man;

but that which cometh out of the mouth,
　　　　this defileth a man."

　　　　　　　　Hence, dimension.
　　If you possess me, I am clean.
　　If I hunger for you,
　　　　　　I am as the stinking flats of a delta.

Nevertheless I hunger.

The grass sings in the parity of its consumption.
　　The lupine,
　　　　　　　the sea-fig are singing,
　　　　　even the Scotch broom is singing

　　its barbarian song.

Jeanette Cemetery

Summer afternoons I could hear
that music, could inquire into the bass
contradiction of things: two alleys, six blocks
and the city to our east
made an invisible map, land-needle
a quilt in its scrolled glove.
Small-numbered depressions in the crabgrass,
enough to turn an ankle. We walked
from class as from a quick spring,
pulsing, the cow raised
with its back to the court,
the old woman allergic to her sun.
In the woods between our house and the arsenal
the ground still lay in old furrows.
You invested in the forest, a production
precise inside its stone system,
a different synopsis.
The cow by itself in its fracture. You said
There is a road where we do not continue,
there was a bright donkey
as there is a rule for the box lid, for the dogleg,
for intelligence—whatever orients—
gilt frontal facade.
And we were learning, we were walking
in the phantoms the leaves had made
relative to cow, to field,
to the age of the summer. Inscribed.
You lived with *N*
where the possible was possible and possibility

seemed necessary, sufficient, just
some dips in the shortcut.
Toscanini, that scientist of the undulant,
I gave away the sketches my body was making.
Which, if applied—if anyone—
breath: blow: impact: sign
deeply deeply.
What the interior of the ghost sees, the lateral
meat of the eye. Light bulb & tin whistle,
they were similar. They were ours.

Feeding the Pear

At the singing someone handed me a pear and said
"Feed it." There was a little mouth drawn on the flank
of the pear, but no nose, no eyes, no ears.
I had no idea what a pear would eat.
I tried carrot sticks. I tried a packet of sugar
from the fellowship hall. The pear remained oblique,
its mouth drawn on, as with magic marker.
The music started up again
but my place on the bench had been taken
by someone else. Anyway I was preoccupied.
I didn't want to bruise the pear. I wanted to be gentle
but I didn't want to advertise my ignorance, either.
There had to be a way.
I started to carry the pear away with me
after the singing was over, after the last of the hymnals
had been closed. "No," someone said, catching
me by the arm. "The pear stays here."

Milton Highway

Currydawn dustworry. A blue tuning as from the south pond in colder weather. Side to side to side to side. Like that. We are pleased. As with the scalp of that other, spider-thin.

Stop.

Side to side to side to side. There is pleasure here. We are shy of union. At the edge of vision: Other. A flapping like a mouth though the smell is iron. This other. Hunger is sufficient, hunger defines.

Periphery scrim: we pass. *Easypickyboypickyboy,* what's called engine overtakes. An offense to hearing.

Another word for *engine* is *martin.* They live in painted gourds. There are three scents to water, one at the back of the throat and one for each naris. None in the engine. None in the gourds.

Doppler of we in the back distance.

Stop.

A long waiting. We remember: stones for the hurting, stones for arranging. Stones between lip & teeth. Carried, as paddock to stall. Oatparley. Hayscent.

He thinks we are alone in this. He thinks that we will eat the stones the way the crusher does. His astonishment. He thinks we are Egyptian.

In fact we see ghosts. This is our sixth cycle. Some know.

Generally we cannot say, generally we are noncommittal. We study surfaces. We confer. We prefer we. Not startle. What he sees as obstinance is not obstinance, it simply. Is. Another; a ghost. One steady motion—

Wither-itch, alfalfa & wild garlic. We make a perfect bride.

Nihil Obstat

For I have gathered the younger parts.
From the clock factories that edge Congress Park—
        "winding ways or indirect proceedings"

    the candle trims this earth
        with its dull finish.

    A festival. As for equinox, though
that date be past: the edging (vast) acquiescence:
      incandescent

            wick

    not least among the cryptographia,
  the cacophilia, the splints & plinths & ambergris.
        Whatsoever was added: say,

    a tread. The bandages
wound tightly onto their steel splines
               like needles,
      the injuries sustained

    in what chalked hospital, between compression
      and the slide, propriety

  (the marble of that unmolested fountain)

gyring feebly forward. We were oilers then,
      the least among brethren.
            And setting out

before the sun had set, weaving
between the tents, pavilions laden
with purchase—and the light beating time,

one petty wage

I should have said. Eidetic. A disturbance
notable chiefly for its hour, rich
declination.   There is a history of patriotism
and of its small particles.
There is no history of night.

Battery Bravo

(first)

One mile, six miles, seventeen:
      the limit of our reach, the tangent
        of our defamation.
   Twenty, thirty.
            Sixty, seventy-five—

Long before the proof
        we understood, intuitively,
    that sound has speed, the space

      between listening and hearing:

   as the ear's whorl
so the hammer, the anvil, path along which
            we step

     one into another.

I wanted to work aboard the dark ship.
I wanted to carry my bouquet
    of checker-lily and wild radish
      and cast it   out
           upon the salt waters,
   far enough

that the tide would wash
          it further, and from this shore.

This was to have been
          my charm against covetousness.

Now I rub these words
          in salt and ochre
                    on this tavern wall.

Once I wrote
          I will be a poet of broken things.
          But what claim have I trampled
                    into these bare hills?
          What fragment have I prised?

I have managed only
                    the sleight of the contrafactum.
          I have risked perjury,
          I have withheld my source; I have denied
                    three times, thirty
                              in the parliament of burnt horses.
          I am the Martha of men,
                    nursing my busy grudge.

Night comes to night as night comes.
          There is no distance between night and *night*
                    as what happens in the night
                              is new, eternally.

Night comes to night as night comes.

With whom shall we be caught up
in the air?

Many of Us Identify with Animals

Half a toy being better than
none. A forest being better than none.
An argot, a pidgin. And the miraculous brevity
of small objects. A broken comb. Detach'd
leg of a beetle. One thinks of children
on their crutches, their encounters with ghosts.
Of all shapes & sizes. Thin branches
of the river myrtles reach through them.
They move in slow groups, as if just returning
from a war. They are trying to believe
something they have forgotten.
Or to make us believe it.
In the same way that the elaborate
miniature landscapes surrounding a model
train set make us believe. In the world outside.
The tucked fields, the milkman and his lantern.
Not so much pinprick. As bezel.
Obtrusion of the syncretic.
Half a quantum being better than.
A history of the papacy during the Renaissance
is very depressing, a friend told me.
Lumps of coal for the boiler smaller than pebbles.
And fitted out. With pine boughs sighing.
With microscopes. Whether zoo or
vitrine. To attract. The approaching children.
Who will remain silent or else cry out
in wonder. Which is it we most long for.
Which is it that they fear.

Cosmologies of the Zinniae

There are periods of talking & not-talking
just as there are periods of eating & not-eating.
The rain falls straight down, into the open windows
and onto the new shirts just received
from Kentucky. They are valiant shirts
and raise their brave sleeves up to the iron mesh.
I am not above calling to them
"Shirts! Though I have not yet worn you
I appreciate your valor and discretion
in this difficult moment." The lead shirt, a nice
periwinkle broadcloth, takes a bow.
What I don't know is that actually
it was stitched by Pentecostals in South Dakota,
not Kentucky. What I never know is
when my life will change, or when the rain will stop
or at least assume a more congenial vector.
One minute there's enough sunlight
to read poems by, the next minute there isn't
and the zinnias in the yard blaze
unconcerned. I am glad for the company
of my nice new shirts, their precise buttonholes.
I am glad for Kentucky, and for South Dakota,
chiefly for what they say about *away*.
The zinnias, of course, are glad for the rain.
There was never anything especially interesting
about the castle: not the drawers
packed with 19th-century stereopticon slides, not even
the secret room with its cabinet of glass eyes.
I catechize my shirts. Like me,

they will grow up to be wary of corridors.
They will strain against the neck & the breastbone.
They will vandalize a prophetic lexicon.
They will never completely dry.

Semble

With all vigor of the saints.
In an upper story.
A fine grain against the wrist like gold stubble.
Is one way we defined time,
then. In that cluster of hive-like houses.
In the corridor of sprung beeves.
And were not ashamed,
or not like that, not in the same way.
Exposed as we were on that shale outcropping.
Supported by an intricate lattice.
Equipped with precision impediments
such as, a hook. Such

as, an eye.
There is such a thing as inheritance,
as a ring sewn into the flesh of the thigh.
So that one can say yes
to the idiocy of
prayer. So that one can profit.
As from experience.
In the nautilus of the skull's ache.
In the friction of the tanager's quick breath.
In the closet of the abandoned icon.
The desert
is a curative process and in that sense
not unlike iodine. The sting,
the pigment.
And the exquisite beaded costumes of the steppes
so carefully preserved.

In the grotto of the declension.
In the rotary of antiquity, of spurious

                              unamaze.
              Ghost of orchard.
                    Or a grate through which the offal flowed.
        There is no figure in the landscape
                              save landscape
      and bees are its crude alphabet.
                    A man with a limp
            tends them. He is not aware of the limp.
  He thinks everyone walks this way.
                              —And what of it?
            What would you tell him?
        In your room at evening, bread,
    wine
              no more than a glass.
In the monastery with its reputation for watchfulness
                  a thief is making off now with gold
                              plates,
      his peeled hands like roses.
            In the heart of the park lies another park.
            In the heart of a sparrow the sun.

Exequy in the Second Mode

I.

Corner swings in the radius of density
suggesting time. Detritus: among the many dialectics

a single coin's edge weds the stained fiber
of sear, (re)visionary amplitude. Nave

as in ship, as in commerce—and lending upward
to worship, spectral tools of like endeavor

cluster, serry. Chipped tooth of the crosscut saw.
Panary of punishment: near diet, proximity

scanned a rough constellation—as ingle,
as fireside—a sleeve for talking *through* the dead.

No geometry but in confluence. And the fiber
transmuted, repayment for Name:

I am an hungered. How recent cities are.
How slender pricked tether to what umber sea.

2.

*"It's easy to feel the poor are blessed
when there are, like, three of them."*
—Steve Grant

Glitter in the faucet, what form am I choosing?
Yclept a necessary hermetick, eye volute

trailed (mixed encampment), vehicle for ebony. Time's
flock affixed: no proscription bears away

from the radial incision. Steep in the discursion
a bridge, unbuilding, pares morning

from drear memory of morning, republic
of some vaster commerce. Artificer of pronouns!

predispose which unguent of the Lake poets
cool from its inhuming. The acid beak, the seedy

monocle rights itself, & saunters. Cold flow
of old oils in a garden of the Louvre.

3.

A glade: personification: *then* the dream,
before any rupture. Nothing wrecks credenza

like architrave, impediment of the plenary.
The rest is space opera. And with the loss of woad

precision's natural caesura, grove of enclosure,
thicket of vessels subject to residence.

We search out the pedigree. I question the sheets:
beneficence of the smallest prophecies, viz.

molecular adulation, the pre-Socratics
& their swilling wicks twin braids gimballed,

ship's compass rendered monument, ∴ broadcast,
an apartment for the poolside of any sprung vacancy;

This is where we live *now*. A fall from event,
fictive net-theft at bedside a-borning.

Ode to the Hottentot Fig

For *sweetness* read *vertigo*, for *beauty* say *pallor.*
There is nothing wrong with the hummingbird's exchange.
If you listen closely you can hear the scuffle of each ant:
they're all Calvinists, they are the architects of small melodies
that flash and tremble in the afternoon sun. Like us,
they demand a more generous explanation.
Conceded, a Jacobin perspective confers a sthenic
vitality on the transmarginal aesthetic elucidated in paragraph five,
proof of the distance between the noumenal
and the recherché. Down by the lighthouse a suspension bridge
replaces the old path over rocks. The seals rejoice:
they know the tide is coming in. Those that are too old
or too sick to care vacation on the mainland like tourists.
All night we hear their somnambulant cries drifting over the lagoon
and in the morning we scry the milky glister
of their dream-tracks in the bougainvillea.
At Battery Wallace someone is playing the French horn.
My body rises like a broken amphora up through each littoral zone.
My immune system is doing just fine.
The bees are sleeping with me: I tie a string to each
so that none fall away in the night. During the small hours
I reconsider the aristocracy of the Euclidean.
Fear is my church key, my gluestick, my Ziploc bag.
I have adapted admirably to this length of rope.
I would rather have been happy in some broken, deserted country.
Here all the clocks have felt in them so they run smoothly.
For *abundance* say *luxate*, for *introduction* read *fall.*

Battery Bravo
(second)

Let us then proclaim
        the new Athens, the new Rome!
We are not the first, but we are worthy.
I would walk with you
        along the colonnades,
                at dusk through the piazzas.

Fact:
        the Nike-Hercules missile
                could achieve speeds above 2.5 mach—
                    altitudes of 4000 feet—
                            in 3.5 seconds.
Guidance system by Bell Labs and Western Electric.
Nitroglycerin-based solid fuel system by Thiokol.
A typical launch facility
        contained two batteries, eight launch pads,
            and employed 135 men.

Fact:
        the main American testing site
            for the Nike-Hercules missile
                was White Sands, in New Mexico.
The main European testing site
        was in Greece.

Did you think it would be so easy, to become free?
How long have you been running?
—And yet we have waited for you.

We are the song you sang in your sleep
when you huddled among furs
on Mt. Tamalpais.
We were the short tips you left
in the cafés of San Francisco.

You look upon the summit of governance,
that acropolis.

Fact:
the Nike-Hercules missile
was designed to ascend to a height of 28 miles.
To seek its target

from above.

There was also, at one time, a matter of dogs.
They were trained here,
they worked, four at a time, four
and each its handler—
German Shepherds mostly.

The men who trained these dogs were sad men.
We can imagine that the men who trained these dogs
were sad men.

Fact:

> when I described these dogs
> as "attack dogs," I was corrected.
>> *Attack dogs are trained to attack,*
>>> the park ranger told me.
>> *These dogs were trained to kill.*

But oh, the glories of this New Rome!
> Of Bell Labs, of Thiokol, of Western Electric!
> Here there shall be no distance.
>> I will say "I am"
>> at the precise moment
>>> you know this to be true.

> And as we have outlawed distance,
>> so we proscribe necessity:

Here there are piers from which no fish are caught.
> Here there are wide avenues
> in which the hooves of horses
>> are no longer heard.
>>> Here

> on the hard clay of tennis courts
> we practice every motion, slowly:
>> Draw the sword.
>>> Return it to its sheath.

Here, we gave the glassblowers every privilege.
Here, we invented a new language for the poets.
Here, we let the artists build museums for themselves.

Do you not yet understand?

There was a myth of our city
            but it has slid from us in a trickle of earth,
                        in the frescoed waters of a fountain.

                        —Do you not yet understand?
(We have been waiting for you.)

Oh, the glories of this New Rome!

Soldier Pass

The sun was bright by the entrance of the mine
and honeybees lit on the white of my white dress shirt
and on the whiter white
of the handle of my denim bag. Some wounds
are made for ministration, that is, healing
as some are white as the white
of a desert flower. These bees would have made a meal of me.
When I walked they took flight, flew

until I stopped again. There is never
enough ore to fill a mine
back up, to staunch the wound. And the bees knew this,
boiling up from the body of a dog
that for some reason had come to rest here, torn
from the apron of the mineshaft beneath a mineral sun.
Like a gas they took their form
from whiteness

which is to say, from excavation,
from absence of flesh, from the white of the eye
I took with me
the way a child pockets a stone
for no good reason, surprised, later, to find it
smooth in his pocket, plain, worthless, useless in its fury.
There was nothing to see, winter thrush
and bracken, the dead

having departed long ago
for Russia else Arcturus. I brushed them from my hair,

from the white of my white shirt,
from the body of the dog.
In the marrow of the long bones of my legs
a sweetness gathered. From the valley, diptych of a single bell.
The dead stood in their corners like silver telescopes.
The bees ferried hunger to their hive.

Habits of the Undertoad

This was the moment I'd been waiting for.
I unlaced my shoes, carefully, and set them by the door.
Outside the ghost of an ancient sea was nosing

among the peaks. A man in a ski mask
was just handing the woman behind the counter
a bolt of blue fabric. Later I would find out

she was my second cousin, twice removed,
but by then consanguinity had been distilled into a qualm.
For too long I had been hesitating between the fifth

and sixth measures of Tallis's *Spem in Alium.*
Something about the self, something about
wanting to hold on. I kept falling out of my century.

Nothing was so simple as feeding pigeons:
I ground the meal for their bread from the carpals
of my left wrist. At night I studied useless subjects

like wheelwrighting and coopering
because I liked the sounds of the names of the tools.
I felt best at night because then the pigeons

were sleeping. Then the woman from behind the counter
would slip into a pair of comfortable shoes
and, by darkness, carry the bolt of blue cloth

back to the terrible house where the man
in the ski mask lived. There was nothing illicit
about this exchange. No laws had been broken.

She would place it gently, almost tenderly,
in the passenger seat of his pedicab. From a distance
it looked almost like a body. From a distance

we can suspect anything is human. A davenport.
A voice vaulting the telegraph wires. A keychain shaped
like a small frog. A pair of orange socks.

Wildwood

The lights come on in the valley below.
When did you last believe shutters were for shutting?
A domestic penance:
these accoutrements, spall and mixed
design breaking like ribbons of speech
on ribbons of water.
Dialect is the truest gift,
self speaking self
the way the trees did,
For we are one yet we are many
and we rise.
There was a time I could not hear
because my ears were stopped with pure honey.
I was standing still.
At what point do thieves cease to steal
our stories, our painted shadows?
—Proverb and joke.
Carefully I copy the image
of empire's currency,
abstraction of the leader, abstraction from the mode:
thus sex as artifact.
Lilith, take heart.
I have not let anyone in.
Scientists now project the pollen count
millennia into the past—
If I refuse to remove my hand from the guiding thread
it is only because I have not yet pledged
allegiance to foreskin, shent villa,
sweet crystal psalm.

Retroactive

—*after Rauschenberg*

I am working against the loom as I have worked against
every good thief, every small tribe, cherubim & seraphim alike
have shown no greater fervor. I delight in the scalpel, the lancet;
I exaggerate the same way a candle in its hubris
deflects yellow from mauve, mauve from black and the wick
like musk, like old sex glowing as if this city were in fact
mine, *pure play of light* and not a small child
pale and bitten in the throat. I will be a poet of broken things.
What I paint white must not be called empty.
This is matrix drawn down to thrust, any transliteration of the vertical
must account for the interruption—slight diagonal tendency—
the float, the play, the drift, genuflection.
Likewise the darkness. I was not dreaming of Oldsmobiles,
I am wide awake; it is my intent to depart intact.
In volition's suburbs the tract houses of my lust go up
one after another. I would not have predicted this particular future.
There is something irresponsible about color
just as there is something irresponsible about maps,
if the circle is a center and the circle is motion
then are we really getting anywhere, caterpillars on a jar's lip
marching until exhaustion takes notice. O wheel.
They have broken the trumpet, its brass shards litter this icy beach.
I am but a peddler of drainboards and dietary supplements.
Without Dottlecob's wax or Dottlecob's awl
I will never achieve a *nuclear family.* Beneath a distant sunrise
my peccadilloes huddle like sheep. Plucked from the circumambient
I will lay down the autoharp of my meticulous ambition
just long enough to set these drapes on fire.

Battery Townsley

Nothing is off limits, now
                    everything is permitted.
       The last gates have been removed.

In the east there is war
       and in the west there is war.
The walls bring news of war
          as they also bring
                  news of love:

RASTAFARI.
     APOCALYPSE <u>NOW</u>
          NO SMOKING
    NOTHING CHANGES, JUST REARRANC
       I DIDN'T DO IT—BUBBY DID.
  LET ME OUT PLEASE.
        THE ARMY IS SO LOGICAL!
      UNITY + SERVICE = RECOVERY
        BRIAN -n- LAURA
              I LOVE YOU.

In time of war the poets turn to war,
   each in his best manner.

I look up, as a dictionary
                    to the living language,
            as a cur to its high table
    I plead for a scrap and am offered the sea.

The hawk and the raven are my wardens,
                    they review every transaction.
    The sun on my face is a bronze coin.

                My steps make a circuit
            as bread makes a circuit.

I am not afraid of the story you ask me to tell.
        (In any case it is no longer
                    my story.)

The lanes of the sea weave brightly
                        in the afternoon sun.
            The buoys toll
                depth, proximity.

Down by Point Reyes
        lie a piece of rock, a chunk of wood
                but I will not go there yet.
        There remains one garment I have not worn.
        There remains my brother,
                whose wounds I have not tended.

There is an eagle branching like a tree
                        in each of my bodies.

There is a grey stone with a white band
in my left cheek.

You must fill me now with your story.

(Once, I too was a child.
—Did you not know?)

Notes

"The Batteries": Each of the nine poems in this sequence is named for and was drafted at the site of one of the nine former gun emplacements at Forts Barry and Cronkhite, demilitarized since 1974 and today part of the Golden Gate National Recreation Area in Marin County, California, just north of San Francisco. Battery Bravo and its companion battery (the former now a museum, the latter housing the California Marine Mammal Hospital) were nuclear missile launch sites during the Cold War. The other batteries contained conventional armaments, were constructed between 1898 and 1944, and were decommissioned immediately following World War II.

All quoted graffiti were actually recorded on-site in April and May, 2003. The Miwok lore recounted in "Battery Smith-Guthrie" comes from *Headlands: The Marin Coast at the Golden Gate,* by Miles Decoster et al. (University of New Mexico Press, 1989). "Battery Townsley" quotes from Thomas McGrath's poem "Ordonnance." The nod at the close of "Battery O'Rorke" is to Mahmoud Darwish.

"City in Search of a Death": San Francisco.

"Circle Park": near Buffalo, Wyoming.

"Bergson's Arrow": The title refers jointly to the French philosopher Henri Bergson (1859–1941) and in turn to Zeno's paradox of the arrow, which Bergson famously glossed.

"Hall of Ancestors": The fourth strophe invokes certain events from Russell Banks's novel *The Darling.*

"Romeward": cf. Acts 27–28.

"Bishopville": located at or near the site of the former Californian mining town of Bodie.

"Jeanette Cemetery": at the junction of Moore and Westmoreland streets in South Boston, Virginia.

"Milton Highway": for my horse, Pick. And for Mark Levine.

"Soldier Pass": in Inyo County, California.

"Habits of the Undertoad": The title, of course, is cribbed from John Irving's *The World According to Garp*.

Acknowledgments

Many thanks to the editors of the publications in which the following poems first appeared, a few in earlier versions:

Boston Review: "Cloud of Witnesses";
Colorado Review: "Battery Alexander," "Soldier Pass";
Conduit: "Transubstantiation Rag";
Crazyhorse: "Habits of the Undertoad," "Milton Highway," "Appanage";
Denver Quarterly: "City in Search of a Death," "Exequy in the Second Mode";
Georgia Review: "Battery Rathbone-McIndoe," "Battery Wallace," "Battery Mendell," "Battery O'Rorke," "Battery Smith-Guthrie," "Battery Bravo" (I & II), "Battery Townsley";
Gettysburg Review: "Feeding the Pear," "Romeward";
Green Mountains Review: "Electuary";
Harvard Review: "Jeanette Cemetery";
Kenyon Review: "Evensong: All Eyes Sharper," "Bergson's Arrow," "Every Apple, Every Dreamer, Every Prime," "Many of Us Identify with Animals";
Mantis: "Nihil Obstat," "Semble";
New England Review: "Blood Ruminant," "The Resurrection: Sweden";
New Orleans Review: "Bishopville," "Circle Park," "Titus at Lystra";
Ninth Letter: "Wildwood," "Ode to the Hottentot Fig," "Hotel d'Avignon";
Pleiades: "Cosmologies of the Zinniae";
Ploughshares: "The Little Man in the Fire Hates Me";
Quarterly West: "Retroactive," "Wunderkammern";
RUNES: A Review of Poetry: "Candlemas, Vermont";
Verse: "What Lived in Our Mouths";
Volt: "Hall of Ancestors."

"Every Apple, Every Dreamer, Every Prime" won the 2005 Cecil Hemley Memorial Award from the Poetry Society of America, judged by

Alice Notley. "Battery Mendell," "Battery O'Rorke," "Battery Bravo" (I & II), and "Battery Townsley" won the 2005 George Bogin Memorial Award from the Poetry Society of America, judged by Joy Harjo. The 9-poem suite "The Batteries" won the 2005 Campbell Corner Poetry Prize.

"Hotel d'Avignon" also appeared in *Legitimate Dangers: American Poets of the New Century*, edited by Michael Dumanis and Cate Marvin (Sarabande, 2006). "The Batteries" appeared as a limited-edition chapbook from New Michigan Press.

Thanks to the Headlands Center for the Arts, the North Carolina Arts Council, the Robert M. MacNamara Foundation, the Atlantic Center for the Arts, the Djerassi Resident Artist Program, and the Corporation of Yaddo; to my parents; and to John Cross, Tony Farrington, Rachel Galvin, Brenda Hillman, Ilya Kaminsky, Brigit Kelly, Paul McCormick, D. A. Powell, Cole Swensen, Arthur Sze, John Yau, and Dean Young. Special thanks to Megan Riley for the Indian pipes of "Candlemas, Vermont."

About the Author

G.C. Waldrep's first collection of poems, *Goldbeater's Skin*, won the 2003 Colorado Prize for Poetry, judged by Donald Revell. His poems have appeared widely in journals, including *Poetry, Ploughshares, Kenyon Review, Gettysburg Review, Boston Review, New England Review, Georgia Review, Colorado Review, Tin House,* and *New American Writing.* His work has received awards from the National Endowment for the Arts, the Poetry Society of America, the Academy of American Poets, the North Carolina Arts Council, and the Campbell Corner Foundation, as well as fellowships at Yaddo, the MacDowell Colony, the Bread Loaf Writers' Conference, and elsewhere.

Waldrep holds degrees in American history from both Harvard and Duke and an MFA in poetry from the University of Iowa. He is also the author of a nonfiction book, *Southern Workers and the Search for Community.* He has taught at Deep Springs College and Kenyon College. Currently he is an assistant professor of English at Bucknell University.

BOA Editions, Ltd.
American Poets Continuum Series

Colophon

Disclamor, poems by G.C. Waldrep, is set in Centaur, a digitalized version of the font designed for Monotype by Bruce Rogers in 1928. The italic, based on drawings by Frederic Warde, is an interpretation of the work of the sixteenth-century printer and calligrapher Ludovico degli Arrighi, after whom it is named.

The publication of this book is made possible, in part, by the special support of the following individuals:

Anonymous (6)
Nancy & Alan Cameros
Gwen & Gary Conners
Susan DeWitt Davie
Peter & Sue Durant
Pete & Bev French
Dane & Judy Gordon
Kip & Deb Hale
Robin & Peter Hursh
Rosemary & Lew Lloyd
Stanley D. McKenzie
Boo Poulin
Deborah Ronnen
Sharon P. Stiller
Judith Taylor
TCA Foundation on behalf of MidTown Athletic Club
Thomas R. Ward in memory of Jane Buell Ward
Mike & Pat Wilder
Glenn & Helen William